DOES GOD EXIST?

building the scientific case

LESSON 1

FAITH **AND** REASON

CAN WE PROVE THE EXISTENCE OF GOD, OR ARE WE LEFT TO GRAPPLE IN THE DARK AND TAKE BLIND LEAPS OF FAITH ABOUT WHAT WE BELIEVE?

OVERVIEW

In this introductory lesson, Dr. Meyer lays out a process to provide reasons for faith by using science and logic to evaluate the great questions of life. In doing so, he is building a case for the existence of God by looking at the evidence all around us.

"I'M GOING TO DO YOU THE DIGNITY OF MAKING AN ARGUMENT!"

DR. STEPHEN MEYER

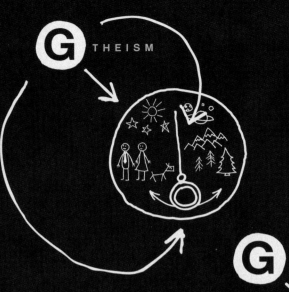

THEISM

DEISM

NATURALISM

PANTHEISM

DIALOGUE

1. What is your definition of FAITH?

2. How do you react to the idea that there is scientific evidence for the existence of God? Why?

3. Besides belief in the personal God revealed in the Bible, what are the other major worldviews?

4. What is the relationship between faith and reason?

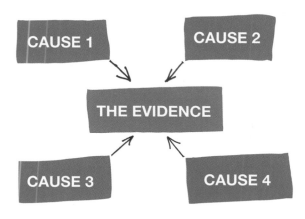

"FOR SINCE THE CREATION OF THE WORLD GOD'S INVISIBLE QUALITIES—HIS ETERNAL POWER AND DIVINE NATURE—HAVE BEEN CLEARLY SEEN, BEING UNDERSTOOD FROM WHAT HAS BEEN MADE."

ROMANS 1:20

LESSON 2

THE BIG BANG COSMOLOGY

"THE HEAVENS DECLARE THE GLORY OF GOD; THE SKIES PROCLAIM THE WORK OF HIS HANDS. DAY AFTER DAY THEY POUR FORTH SPEECH; NIGHT AFTER NIGHT THEY DISPLAY KNOWLEDGE."

PSALM 19:1-2

Is the universe infinite, *or did it have an actual beginning ("finite")? Why should we care? In this lesson, Dr. Meyer provides the opening arguments for a finite universe by studying the expansion rate of the cosmos.*

Richard Dawkins and the other "new atheists" argue against this notion, believing the universe had no beginning and will have no end. If they were right, there would be no place for God. However, if the universe had a first cause, or beginning, then what was that cause? The answer appears to point toward a transcendent force that acted outside of space and time, leading us to believe our universe had a distinct beginning.

infinite or finite?

"I NOW SEE THE NECESSITY OF A BEGINNING."

ALBERT EINSTEIN

"This is an exceedingly strange development, unexpected by all but the theologians. They have always accepted the word of the Bible: In the beginning God created heaven and earth. . . . It is unexpected because science has had such extraordinary success in tracing the chain of cause and effect backward in time. For the scientist who has lived by his faith in the power of reason, the story ends like a bad dream. He has scaled the mountains of ignorance; he is about to conquer the highest peak; as he pulls himself over the final rock, he is greeted by a band of theologians who have been sitting there for centuries."

ROBERT JASTROW, ASTRONOMER

DIALOGUE

1. What are the two competing theories surrounding the cause of the universe?

2. Where have you encountered the "new atheism" in your academic, social or spiritual life? What impact has it had on your faith?

3. What did scientists believe about the universe before Hubble discovered that it is expanding?

4. If the universe truly had a beginning, explain how that helps us answer the question, Does God exist?

"SIRE, I HAVE NO NEED OF THAT HYPOTHESIS."

PIERRE LAPLACE

03

"IN MY VIEW THE QUESTION OF ORIGIN SEEMS ALWAYS LEFT UNANSWERED IF WE EXPLORE FROM A SCIENTIFIC POINT OF VIEW ALONE. THUS, I BELIEVE THERE IS A NEED FOR SOME RELIGIOUS OR METAPHYSICAL EXPLANATION. I BELIEVE IN THE CONCEPT OF GOD AND IN HIS EXISTENCE."

CHARLES TOWNES, NOBEL LAUREATE

LESSON 3

THE BIG BANG COSMOLOGY,

PART 2

"THERE WAS A TIME WHEN TIME BEGAN."

DR. STEPHEN MEYER

"SOMETHING MUST BE THE THING FROM WHICH EVERYTHING ELSE COMES."

DR. STEPHEN MEYER

OVERVIEW

Once upon a time, *in a universe far, far away. . . . Wait, this isn't a fairy tale; we're talking about reality. If you and I could go back far enough in time, we would come to a point when the universe did not exist. But if the universe truly had a distinct beginning, then what caused the cosmos to come into existence? According to Dr. Meyer, the Big Bang theory best accounts for the overwhelming evidence regarding the origin of the universe. But the Big Bang (or "first effect" of the universe) requires a "first cause." So what caused the Big Bang? Dr. Meyer contends that, based on the evidence, theism has the most convincing answer. Naturalism and pantheism both fail to provide a cause that could bring the cosmos into existence.*

"IF YOU ARE TALKING ABOUT THE
ORIGIN OF SPACE AND TIME ITSELF,
YOU NEED SOMETHING THAT EXISTS
OUTSIDE OF SPACE AND TIME."

DR. STEPHEN MEYER

DIALOGUE

1. Why does the Big Bang theory have theological implications?

2. Why is it important to think of the Big Bang as an "effect" of the universe rather than the "cause" of the universe?

3. In light of the evidence for the Big Bang theory, what are the basic shortcomings of other explanations for the origin of the universe?

4. In your own words, why does a theistic explanation of the origin of the cosmos seem to make the most sense?

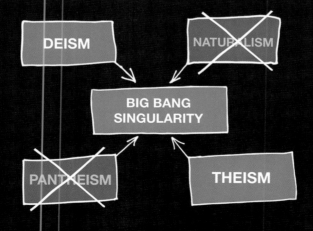

"A COMMONSENSE INTERPRETATION OF THE DATA SUGGESTS THAT A SUPERINTELLECT HAS MONKEYED WITH PHYSICS, AS WELL AS WITH CHEMISTRY AND BIOLOGY."

SIR FRED HOYLE, COSMOLOGIST

LESSON 4

THE BIG BANG COSMOLOGY,

PART 3

"WE LIVE IN THE 'JUST RIGHT' UNIVERSE."

DR. STEPHEN MEYER

OVERVIEW

In this lesson, Dr. Meyer introduces the "anthropic fine-tuning principle," highlighting evidence that the universe runs according to specific, intelligent laws of physics and cosmology that allow life to exist. If the universe looks finely tuned for life, then maybe there was a Fine-Tuner, someone who set up those life-sustaining parameters.

The materialistic worldview has significant problems with this theory, so who is right? Is it mere chance that life came into existence? Was life simply necessary? Or does the fine-tuning principle demand an intelligent source acting outside the space-time universe? Let's let the evidence lead us to the answers.

"THE THOUGHT INSISTENTLY ARISES THAT SOME SUPERNATURAL agency—OR, RATHER, Agency— MUST BE INVOLVED. IS IT POSSIBLE THAT SUDDENLY, WITHOUT INTENDING TO, WE HAVE STUMBLED UPON SCIENTIFIC PROOF OF THE EXISTENCE OF A SUPREME BEING? WAS IT GOD WHO STEPPED IN AND SO PROVIDENTIALLY CRAFTED THE COSMOS FOR OUR BENEFIT?"

GEORGE GREENSTEIN, ASTRONOMER

DIALOGUE

1. What are some of the ways the universe has been fine-tuned to support human life?

2. How does the "fine-tuning" argument support belief in the intelligent design of the universe?

3. How have scientists tried to explain away the fine-tuning of the universe?

4. Do you believe intelligent design is the best explanation of the origin of the universe? Why or why not?

"THE UNIVERSE IS A SET-UP JOB."

DR. STEPHEN MEYER

05

"THE MACHINE CODE OF THE GENES IS UNCANNILY COMPUTER-LIKE. APART FROM DIFFERENCES IN JARGON, THE PAGES OF A MOLECULAR BIOLOGY JOURNAL MIGHT BE INTERCHANGED WITH THOSE OF A COMPUTER ENGINEERING JOURNAL."

RICHARD DAWKINS

LESSON 5

DNA BY DESIGN

OVERVIEW

The question of design *is a critical worldview-shaping paradox. If biology points us to the appearance of design, then what are we to make of it? Darwinian evolutionists believe that the scientific explanation for the appearance of design is natural selection, or "undirected causes." Simply put, they believe the design we observe is only an illusion.*

However, significant evidence for intelligent design is found in the inner workings of the cell and in the complex makeup of DNA. It is becoming more and more apparent that theism provides the best explanation for the phenomena of design and information in the cells of all living things.

"HUMAN DNA IS LIKE A COMPUTER PROGRAM BUT FAR, FAR MORE ADVANCED THAN ANY WE'VE EVER CREATED."

BILL GATES

"THE CELL IS A SIMPLE HOMOGENOUS GLOBULE OF PLASM."

T. H. HUXLEY, 1869

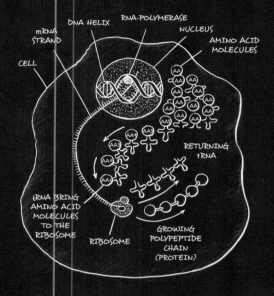

- mRNA STRAND
- DNA HELIX
- RNA-POLYMERASE
- NUCLEUS
- AMINO ACID MOLECULES
- CELL
- RETURNING tRNA
- tRNA BRING AMINO ACID MOLECULES TO THE RIBOSOME
- RIBOSOME
- GROWING POLYPEPTIDE CHAIN (PROTEIN)

WHAT IS THE FUNDAMENTAL MYSTERY OF LIFE?

D I A L O G U E

1. From your perspective, why is the COMPLEXITY of the information in DNA so important in thinking about the most likely explanation for the origin of life?

2. Why is the SPECIFICITY of the information in DNA also so important?

3. Why do you think many scientists seem determined to explain the origin of life without reference to God?

4. What one area in the design argument do you still have doubts about? Why?

06

"MAYBE WE ARE LOOKING AT SOMETHING THAT APPEARS DESIGNED BECAUSE IT REALLY IS DESIGNED."

DR. STEPHEN MEYER

LESSON 6

DNA BY DESIGN,

PART 2

"THERE IS NO NATURALISTIC EXPLANATION FOR THE ORIGIN OF THE INFORMATION THAT YOU NEED TO BUILD THE FIRST LIFE."

DR. STEPHEN MEYER

Is it possible for life to have begun by mere chance? Where did the specified information in DNA come from? How did life first begin? Chance, natural selection and self-organization are three hypotheses that have been postulated by naturalistic scientists to explain the origin of life.

However, Dr. Meyer shows the mathematical and logical difficulties in explaining the origin of life using any of these three theories. The conclusion is inescapable: undirected processes do not create the information needed to produce life.

Odds of Getting Combination by Chance

150 sites with **20** amino acids = 20^{150}

Over 10^{195} possible combinations!

Probabilistic Resources of the Universe

$$10^{80}$$
(elementary particles) X

$$10^{16}$$
(seconds since Big Bang) X

$$10^{43} = 10^{139}$$
*(maximum number of interactions
between elementary particles)*

1. In general, what are the odds against life—or even a single protein—coming into existence by mere chance? How convincing was Dr. Meyer's argument?

2. What is meant by "self-organization," and why does this theory fail to account for the arrangement of information in DNA?

3. Summarize how this lesson bolsters the argument for the intelligent design of life.

"THE CREATION OF NEW INFORMATION IS HABITUALLY ASSOCIATED WITH CONSCIOUS ACTIVITY."

HENRY QUASTLER

LESSON 7

DNA BY DESIGN,
PART 3

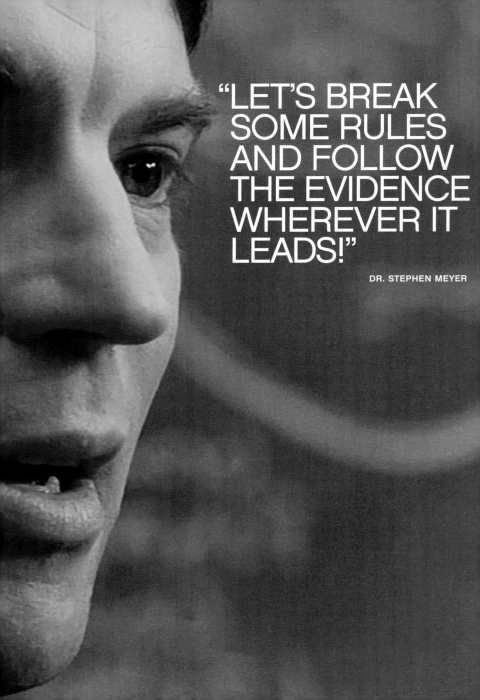

"LET'S BREAK SOME RULES AND FOLLOW THE EVIDENCE WHEREVER IT LEADS!"

DR. STEPHEN MEYER

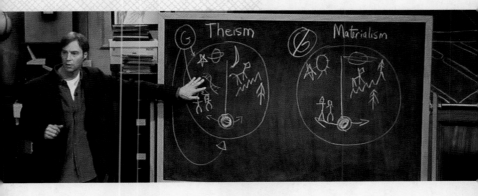

OVERVIEW

A fundamental rule of the modern scientist is that no non-naturalistic (or supernatural) concepts can be employed to explain the origin of life. Therefore, the debate regarding the origin of life is not just about the evidence itself, but also about the presuppositions that keep the scientist from considering all possible explanations.

We know that the source of any and all information found within the DNA code is intelligence itself. So where does this intelligence come from? Chance? Natural selection? Dr. Meyer has shown already that those hypotheses do not hold water. Therefore, the most plausible source of information within the universe is an intelligent designer, pointing us toward a transcendent Creator of the universe.

"WHEN WE FIND INFORMATION IN A DNA MOLECULE, ENCODED IN DIGITAL FORM, THE MOST **LOGICAL** CONCLUSION IS THAT THE INFORMATION HAD AN INTELLIGENT SOURCE."

DR. STEPHEN MEYER

DIALOGUE

1. What is meant by intelligence in nature? What two components are needed to assume "design"?

2. What is "junk DNA"? Why is it not really junk?

3. How does "methodological naturalism," or a bias against anything involving God, limit a scientist's ability to seek out the true origin of life?

4. How would you discuss intelligent design with a naturalistic or materialistic professor?

08

"HE HAS CAUSED HIS WONDERS TO BE REMEMBERED."

PSALM 111:4

LESSON 8

THE RETURN
OF THE
GOD
HYPOTHESIS

OVERVIEW

When one takes *all the evidence into*
account, from the fine-tuning of the
universe to the source of information
itself, to the finite beginning of the
universe and the mathematical genius
of digital code, there is a compelling
case to be made for the existence
of God. In fact, it may be the only
intelligent theory left standing—the best
plausible explanation for the origin of
the universe and life itself.

"MAGNA OPERA DOMINI
EXQUISITA IN OMNES
VOLUNTATES EJUS."

("GREAT ARE THE WORKS OF THE LORD, SOUGHT OUT BY ALL WHO
TAKE PLEASURE THEREIN." PSALM 111:2)

"EXQUISITE TECHNOLOGY IS WORKING RIGHT NOW IN THE MITOCHONDRIA OF YOUR CELLS."

DR. STEPHEN MEYER

DIALOGUE

1. In review, what are some key evidences Dr. Meyer points to that lead us to theism? How convincing is his argument?

2. What has changed in the last three hundred years that makes the theistic worldview even more plausible as the best explanation for the universe?

3. What is the Cambrian explosion? How does it provide credence to the theistic worldview? And what about other recent discoveries?

09

LESSON 9

THE MORAL NECESSITY OF THEISM

"IF GOD DOES NOT EXIST, EVERYTHING IS PERMITTED."

ATTRIBUTED TO FYODOR DOSTOEVSKY

OVERVIEW

It is impossible to live as a moral relativist. Everyone believes in some standard of right and wrong, but what is that standard and where did it come from? In this lesson, Dr. Meyer moves away from science and cosmology to discuss the philosophical and ethical arguments for the existence of God. Without God, how can we distinguish right from wrong? In fact, Meyer points out that "only if you believe in God can you give a sensible account of what it means for something to be right or wrong."

"IF GOD DID NOT
EXIST, IT WOULD BE
NECESSARY TO
INVENT HIM."

VOLTAIRE

DIALOGUE

1. Why is it so difficult to live as a moral relativist—to deny the existence of any objective moral standard?

2. Is there an intrinsic, qualitative difference between human beings and animals? What sorts of things happen when a society denies that people are made in the image of God?

3. How do you determine right from wrong? What do you think of the idea that we have no freedom to choose and can't be held responsible for our actions?

LESSON 10

THE MORAL NECESSITY OF THEISM,

PART 2

OVERVIEW

In this capstone lesson, Dr. Meyer provides overwhelming evidence that the theistic worldview, rather than relativism or evolutionary ethics, is the only one that can provide a coherent explanation for an objective and meaningful system of morality.

Finally, by studying the actions of all human beings, we see that everyone points to an objective moral code, and the best explanation for the source of that code is the existence of God. He provides the only explanation for any transcendent standard of morality and ethics.

"THE TRUTH IS, EITH
THERE **IS** A GOD C
THERE **ISN'T**."

DIALOGUE

1. How does not believing in God lead to situational or relative ethics? On the other hand, how does the theistic worldview help us determine right from wrong?

2. What are some practical ways in which you can engage a relativistic friend or professor concerning his or her core beliefs? What are some things such a person can't say or do?

3. Evolutionary ethicists believe that natural selection has allowed human beings to develop a system of morality and ethics. Does this hypothesis make sense? How would you go about debunking this theory?

4. After participating in these ten lessons, what new or stronger "reasons for your faith" do you now have?

"YOUR WORLD-VIEW HAS TO HAVE THE SAME SHAPE THAT REALITY DOES."

J. BUDZISZEWSKI

Stephen C. Meyer is Senior Fellow at the Discovery Institute outside of Seattle, Washington. He has spent twenty years researching cosmology, biology and metaphysics to determine the existence of a creator God. Steve received his Ph.D. from Cambridge University and is author of SIGNATURE IN THE CELL: DNA AND THE EVIDENCE FOR INTELLIGENT DESIGN.

Dave Stotts, host and editor of the Drive Thru History series, has been working with Jim Fitzgerald and ColdWater Media since 2001. His twelve years working in Christian media production have taken him to twenty-seven countries to shoot and edit award-winning documentaries. Dave lives in Dallas, Texas, with his wife, Rebekah, and their children.

Gary Alan Taylor is the senior manager for Focus on the Family's The Truth Project and the owner of TrueU. He has been associate director of admissions for the Focus on the Family Institute and worked in administration at Milligan College in Johnson City, Tennessee. Gary Alan holds advanced degrees in European and American history and is an affiliate faculty member of the history department at Colorado Christian University.